WITCH

Rebecca Tamás was born in London and currently lives in York, where she lectures at York St John University. Rebecca is the editor, with Sarah Shin, of the anthology *Spells: Occult Poetry for the 21ˢᵗ Century* (Ignota Press, 2018). She has published three pamphlets of poetry: *The Ophelia Letters* (Salt, 2013), *Savage* (Clinic, 2017) and *Tiger* (Bad Betty Press, 2018). *WITCH* is her first full-length collection.

@RebTamas

WITCH

Rebecca Tamás

Penned in the Margins
LONDON

PUBLISHED BY PENNED IN THE MARGINS
Toynbee Studios, 28 Commercial Street, London E1 6AB
www.pennedinthemargins.co.uk

The right of Rebecca Tamás to be identified as the author of this work has been asserted by her in accordance with Section 77 of the Copyright, Designs and Patent Act 1988.

First published 2019

Printed in the United Kingdom by TJ International

ISBN
978-1-908058-62-1

CONTENTS

ACKNOWLEDGEMENTS

A number of the poems in *WITCH* appeared in earlier forms in the publications *The White Review*, *The Poetry Review*, *The Suburban Review*, *Magma*, *Minerva Platform*, *Funhouse Magazine*, *The London Review of Books*, *Poetry London*, *Frieze Magazine*, *The Rialto*, *Test Centre*, *Poetry Wales*, Five Leaves Bookshop's 'Postcard Poems' for National Poetry Day, in the anthology *The World Speaking Back ... To Denise Riley* (Boiler House Press, 2018) and in the pamphlet *Savage* (Clinic, 2017).

Thank you to Arts Council England and The Fenton Arts Trust for their support whilst developing and writing this book.

To my friends

WITCH

A woman like that is not a woman, quite.
I have been her kind.

ANNE SEXTON

§

What differs from the existent will strike the
existent as witchcraft.

THEODOR ADORNO

/penis hex/

the hex for a penis isn't really all about
the penis
the penis is not an issue all fine doing its own thing
ink blot semen   sweet white plaster
pale peach tartlet
but when it goes you see   you see a lot of things

to hex a penis off means taking a laugh out for a walk
long and blue
cold as Russia
laughing and laughing your mouth is open
let your girlfriend see your tongue

to hex a penis off wrap yourself up
in a warm bed and no one is there
intellectual persuasion
hand in the unowned air
peeling strips of dull bleached sky

hex like artemisia
holofernes' head back   the fucking sucker
head back and tirades full of blood
he goes down way way down
judith's painted hand is a snare
she is catching your penis and taking it home

hex with a plate of grilled pears
against cream
a glass of just-pink wine
teacups porcelain thrush egg blue
your soft under the breath singing

hex it off with a little journey
islands of any kind ideally somewhere cold
green things butting out into a black/grey sea
no one is on the island to tell you the kind of
things you should be touching

hex at a child-wedding
don't worry it's cool
at the ceremony just wait until the
drinks are being served and then set fire

to the whole place
the drapes that are azure blue
holiday destination   blue pope innocent blue
the child-bride comes with you
her big gobstopper eyes and hello kitty backpack
full of dicks

hex in a philosophy seminar
see them start to detach and waver
a few centimetres apart from their owners

maybe I'm not actually bothered by the logical
summation of things
their soft and sweet calculation and steadfast rationale
maybe I like it out here in the dark cold wood
with all my bits hanging down and fiery creatures
perching on every surface shaking their claws
maybe I like it with god holding my sweaty wavering hand

hex it by saying nothing
this navy zip-up and scarf says that I understand comfort
and solidarity
don't talk to me   don't tell me about your day

or ask me where the good places are
is there a problem is this sector
no
off it goes

turn back and unpave the roads
hex an epic poem   some kind of discharge
a throne that you forged from
gold and diamonds and plastic bangles
and crow feathers and infinity rings

hex it through glory
total and utter glory
your huge red/black hair reaching and touching the upper
        echelons
pagan understanding and all types of weird singing
some woman in a mint silk pantsuit so happy with
a penis between her legs and the next shucking it off
able to do exactly as is necessary

wind batters the tall insane skyscrapers
glowering hungry sky   very unusual
that metallic taste in your mouth
it's changing   you see

Interrogation (1)

Are you a witch?

Are you

Have you had relations with the devil?

Have you

Have you had relations with the devil and what took place?

I kissed him under the tail, it was a bit like soil, a bit like road tar
when it heats up, he was flickering in pleasure, the field would
be just the same when I tongue that, the bird's feathers parting.

What knowledge did the devil give you?

I built a house near to the sea, the roof is red/orange, the sky
is a shaking plate of light peeling you back, there is grass
out the front, some metal bins, you can see a lighthouse. I began

to sleep with the windows open, I began to creep along the bed
to my own globe face in the mirror. Sitting rubbed up in myself
is this fierce fire, it does not come from me, even the stones in
the drive are crackling with it.

What did the devil make you do under his control?

His mother had just died. We ate mint ice
cream by the coffin, he was missing her, my
sock was loose, we kept laughing.

What is magic?

Picture an egg yolk, that huge yellow throw-up sun.
Dementedly shining, falling out of itself, birthed and
reverent.

What is magic?

Little cracks coming in, small flaws in the glass,
and the air slapping itself, you stand on a hill,
things are mainly green and breakable,
you think ok I'm not alone, but mainly,

ok I was never alone, on a far-off hill the
earth is breaking up against the gas pressure
of the sun, if there was ever anything to miss
this is what you miss, how it's beginning.

What crimes have you enacted?

Love makes me forget myself sometimes.
I am horribly angry, I am sick with it,
my vomit turns black, but this love.
I can't explain it, beyond that it is exactly.

What other witches/sorcerers have you conjured with?

S couldn't eat. The food was poor and cheap but not that.
She had these amazing dark eyes.

Have you taken black mass?

I've wondered why things turn. Rustling and fluttering cells,
the nib of the chest where what you might call soul slides out
and enters a hyena fucking happily amongst the fruit rinds.

What did the devil make you do under his control?

What you should do is go out and get really drunk.

What did the devil make you do under his control?

What you should do is get a sleeper train.

What did the devil make you do under his control?

I can pack everything and I can carry the suitcases up
staircases and along roads. I can go, even though
I am not, importantly, myself. Some of the things
that are within me can go.

Have you profaned holy scripture?

The biggest fear is that reality itself starts to curdle,
stiffens into waxy stops.

Were you born to witches or trained in witchcraft?

Were you

Who have you used spells against in this parish?

I can't say that I've met god face to face, but I
can tell you how I imagine it. God holding my heart
in a palm as it flexes from blue to green to white.
God being really tired, haar of sea fog.
I've had to decide what it looks like, what it is.
Shiver of the long world, cold feet,
a small, bright, filthy song.

WITCH AND THE DEVIL

when the witch first met the devil the devil was
a beautiful man and a beautiful woman
the devil had long eyelashes and a body that was hard and soft
at the same time so that you wanted to hold him
and also be held by her and run your hands through the curly
sticky liquorice hair which smelt of the salt churned up by the
    prow of a boat
the devil wanted to know the witch he wanted to ask about the
    spells she did
when she pulled roots out of the living air and controlled
    jackdaws with the ease
of directing first-year undergraduates in a department play
he wanted to see the things she could do when she pushed her
    fingers into the mud
and listened as best she could to what the mud was saying until
    sometimes the mud
found its way up her throat and out of her mouth
the devil was very different the witch could see he was different
    by the way he talked

to her and actually listened to the answers
the witch liked his sloping gait and the way he looked at
      her with oilslick eyes
that kept changing colour sky and sea shifting direction
the witch had been waiting for a long time because even though
she lived in a pre-industrial society she dreamt of motorways
      and nightclubs
though she didn't know they were called motorways and nightclubs
she dreamt of huge chunks of the sky falling down and
covering all the spires
drowning all the bells and towns and ploughs and churches
      in blue

the devil liked getting up early which is what the witch
      liked so they would go out
before anyone else was around and they would act out
      satanic rituals in the woods
the witch was surprised by this because she thought the
      devil would prefer the night-time
but she was also pleased because you could see what you
      were doing a lot better at dawn
and also the light had the green tint of rusted copper and
      took part in the celebrations

which the devil said were the best he had probably ever done
    because the witch was so
good at doing them and such a natural
the witch kept having sex with the devil and the devil
    had all the sexual organs you could
want so the witch could have him inside her at the same
    time as putting his breast in her mouth
and even though the witch had always assumed that she
    probably did like sex in general
though not usually in practice this time the witch liked it
    in practice because she didn't have
to put her hand over her mouth or anything like that she
    just had to do what she was doing
and the devil loved putting his tongue between her and
    also turning into other animals whilst he was
down there so the witch didn't just feel like she was getting
    what she wanted she felt like everyone
everywhere was getting what they wanted

the devil made the witch a salad which had lettuce and
    cucumber in it but which also had
watermelon in it the pink flesh and the black seeds
the witch began crying at this though she wasn't exactly

clear why

something about the wet pinkness and hard blackness and
the cold fruit of it in her mouth

against the slightly dirty vegetables reminded her of the
descriptions of Christ's resurrection

when after all that time behind a boulder being dead he
comes out and he is still dead but

he's alive at the same time and is glowing with an odd light
like a northern summer when

the sun doesn't set and he's smiling in his whole but also
destroyed flesh

which is staying on his bones with the pink new blood
that someone put in there

the witch showed the devil how to talk through eye blinks
so that no one else

knew what was going on and the devil tried to show the
witch how to become

invisible but that was a really hard one that was going to
take her a while to get right

the devil had a lot of books with him which he kept
stuffed in his underwear drawer

a mix of things like the bible told backwards and general

works of contemporary literature
so the witch could read all of that when she wasn't
    practising how to change the weather
by sucking on a spoon of honey and dog hair or how to
    use parsley to stop the
pastor speaking on sundays so that he would just have to
    wave his hands around and try
and impersonate the terrible fires of hell and the scalding
    water that would greet each sinner
when they finally gave up their hard life and went onto the
    next hard life for another go

the witch had never thought about what other people
    thought about exactly
she had thought about those motorways and nightclubs
    and had imagined getting run
over or dying of a drug overdose she had also imagined
    turning to chalk and dissipating
she had imagined giving birth to a huge squadron of frogs
    and eels
and she had told people about it which meant that she
    didn't have to worry about getting
married as much as other girls or women or young men

had to worry about getting married
but now she was thinking about different different things
    like unrolling clouds of blue tits
from the cavities between her muscles and a huge ornate
    building filled with beds so that you
couldn't see the floor only lovely silk-topped mattresses
    where women climbed from bunk to bunk
whispering to each other and lighting candles and never
    having to have their feet touch the sawdust
under a roof made of clear glass so that they could all see
    out but no one could see in

the devil didn't like to talk about god that much because
    of their falling out
the witch wasn't even sure sometimes if the devil 100%
    believed in him
still the witch wanted to know what god was like from a
    being with first-hand experience
she wanted to unplug the gap that she had thought about
    at night when she was small
thinking of nothing praying to nothing watching the
    curtain slap and slap against the window
so the devil described a landscape of ice with icy crags and

peaks rising up into an ice pale sky
vast expanses of snow tunnelling along wind channels in
        twisted curls and icebergs wide and
huge as continents bleeding water down onto the frozen
        sheets of ice which were too thick
to be tested with scientific instruments air that is so cold
        that birds that fly into it are knocked down dead
straight away whales are left cubed and shattered as
        they meet the immobile sea
miles and miles of whiteness so that looking at it is also
        not looking at it the witch asked how can god be
an environment made of ice and the devil said no god isn't
        the ice he's under the ice
but you have to be very very very hot to burn your way
        through to him

one thing the witch didn't ask the devil about was badness
        even though she knew a lot
of people would say that the devil was full of badness if
        not defined by badness
but by this point the witch was as sick of goodness
        as she was sick of badness
in fact she was really sick of them her spine ached with all

of it collecting

like pink nauseous liquid in the links between her vertebrae

the witch wanted some sort of power though she knew it
would get her into trouble

the witch wanted to be allowed to do her own thing
without disturbance

she wanted to throw the broom into the grate and instead

buy an airplane rising across a tin-can-silver sky higher and
higher

30,000 feet and rising so high that no one can grab onto
your ankles

no one can cover you or take a shot get you on your back
pull something

a blue void of cloud cold planets shoals of birds

she had always been looking up so had been practising for
a long time

standing on ledges craning her neck and picturing a space
outside the ground

a walk into the air that looks like the future because it is

the devil said that he was accused of murder wherever he
went even though

he never murdered anybody not because of morality but for

other reasons

to do with essential life force and the energy capture of the seasons

he said he wasn't a man and wouldn't drink milk because it didn't
belong to him and that

even if someone was with him for 1,000 years they weren't going
to get him

there was nothing to get or at least getting doesn't work like that

the devil did say he believed in a personal kind of sacrifice that
didn't involve

an altar or necessarily have a particular cause though he had a
soft spot for martyrs

he rather said that you had to make a decision are you prepared
to destroy yourself

for freedom even though it will be really awful and maybe worse
than not freedom

even though it will involve some true horror examples of

which include lungs full of swamp tar

the smallest bit of daylight refracting through permanently shut
blinds

and a large selection of types of silence each and every one of
which are unobserved

the devil always looked at the witch with an expression of
compassion which was

the same expression she had on her face when she looked at him
but when he talked about freedom he looked painfully quiet
    like the kind of
person who casts no shadow and the witch wondered if actually
    that was because
her face looked like that

when the witch said goodbye to the devil
they didn't get overtly emotional but they held onto each other
for a long time until there was a flow of breath back and forth
that was entirely equal in the air passing through their mouths
it is terrible how we can never guarantee anything we really want
is what the witch thought but still she took a bit of her hair and
    tied it round
the devil's wrist and the devil said something in her ear but it
    wasn't words
so I can't transcribe it but it looked like a body floating on a sea
of grass with the moon pulling that grass backwards and forwards
in tides and with each tug of the moonlight more blue flowers
    burst up
out of the soil and stretch their capped mouths and the
body passes over them
in light so strong you could read by it

WITCH AND THE SUFFRAGETTES

again somehow the witch finds it is about eating and not eating
they don't eat and so they are made to eat
she asks a policeman 'what is with this eating thing?'
but he doesn't know why just that when a woman eats
she is eating for the state
when she watches her friend forced to lie back and be fed
she retches
the feeding is the same as being sick it is the same as not
being fed because it leaves you hungry
ghost meal fattened with air
the witch tries to listen to the feeding because it is saying
something
she knows it looks like a penis being forced down her throat
and she knows that they know it
the feeding wants to make things happen without desire
weakness is too close to permeability
see-through bones which are an obvious lack
calling out EMPTY EMPTY EMPTY EMPTY body only
small because the mind is small there is no room for it inside

the feeding is the Tipp-Ex and it says that fullness is the cover-up
when the witch is fed she thinks how interesting it is that
fullness can be so blank
groping around in the sick dark not allowed to pour out only
allowed to take in

the witch is sad when she thinks about the suffragettes
their pale green and pink their soft bodies and hard placards
the witch wonders what happiness could possibly look like
at some point it went wrong and even though she's very old
she doesn't know exactly when that point was
but she's thinking that the most likely is probably Orpheus
when Orpheus was singing it was so marvellous and Eurydice
        sang too
obviously they were a really good couple
back then it was early you could still smell the cinders coming
        off the big bang
nothing had really fixed yet nothing looked lasting
trees were improvising their places
Orpheus went back to get Eurydice from death as we know
but he wouldn't let her make her own way out of the rubble
        seek into the scratch of
each step that is not knowing always not knowing

he looked at her eyes which were dry and dark
her song is still down there somewhere

the smell of freedom is the smell of vomit the witch can see
        that now
it isn't lots of clear light pouring in gold fantastic gold
it is vomiting all over yourself and it getting hard in the folds
it is getting your time and they don't give you anything so
you bleed down your legs thighs sticky
so they smack when you move them wet gloss
smell of slaughtered animals the unclean things
is the smell of where you're going into the sweat
of piss and cold
into the rawness where the inside comes outside
which is exactly what they hate
the smell of earth is like this
it's dirty

the rush of death is a stunt
it vibrates its own meaning
which garbles and surpasses you
all of the explosions are coming
out of your head eating the words

when the houses burn are you meant
to feel sorry for it the witch thinks probably
yes but obviously no
all the fires coursing up the townhouses
and golf courses and morning rooms and
nurseries and halls of commerce and residences
were all already there cracking and flailing
and spitting
the pleasure of seeing everyone see it
their white eyes fat with flames
it is all burning it has all been burning us

WITCH SCOLD

she looked at the hard bridle
saw it running with its own capture
red and
blue and
black
stop
witch attempted to be separate from her own body
witch attempted to unwoman
witch was not a wife but they could hear her going on
and on and on and wow and on
he held her arms and she kicked and someone else did
it went over her head the metal bar over her tongue
caged latches she stopped struggling she could not get away
so she made her eyes black holes dragging gravity
the tongue's flesh was spongy and wet it was raining
so in the marketplace of course she waited one arm
tied to a post and all of that metal on her head her brain
people did their early capitalist accumulation
people said things and there was no saying back

now there were no words that words should break
and if a kind of silence was home what vocabulary
could be eaten back could be swallowed new names
in the damp thought-spaces where no noise comes
a loud cry that isn't the name of a cry but is a cry
there was a small group of people left in a forest
she had heard their language was a collection
of bird sounds in the sounds time did not exist
there were no names the canopy opened like a huge mouth
running speaking through itself with a burning fork
words until they burn and scald insufficient
from far away witch could see a ship moving
it was taking voices in soot boxes
the sails were white so she knew pain
because of course standing there the tongue
death was white and not black death had always
been white waving its blank lock into the air
its jargon from a capped and stained spreadsheet

WITCH GOVERNMENT

the witch thinks about what it would be like to fuck the
    government
the government would be an octopus would it or no a giant squid
that huge cobalt industrial complex eye
how can anything be that big
how can basically a prawn swell and swell to these Cousteau
    proportions
you can't see where its sex parts are you can only see the eye the huge
impossible eye much more sophisticated than an X-ray
which only sees bones this sees soul this sees sin this sees your
    GPS location
the fucking happens without visibility there are things touching
    the insides of you
perhaps its huge phallus has entered you and is moving around
    but then again
it could be one of the tentacles and you don't have any way of
    knowing
there must be pornos a lot like this but with slightly less rare
    animals

unsurprisingly witch thinks it would not be nice in the
    traditional sense of nice
the pulsating tentacles or phallus or phalluses breaking into
    different sections of
your body as if you are an unpicked thread material meeting
    material slowly
taking the speech bits and the feelings bits and uncoring them
    like slit avocados
discarding and melting down and widening into a colossal shouting
on the other hand there are some elements that want absolutely
    no resistance at all
that want to slick and shuddering the parts that hurt gone and
    vomited
it is horrifying but easy it doesn't take effort forcing yourself to
    watch a bad film
but just happens the brine flow and the thick parts soldering
    into your vagina
your own eye is closed your own breath is making sympathies
    saying let's stay healthy
or somewhere out in the sea I found myself and melted into this
    everything
even though the fucking is deeply impersonal and separate each
    breast a round cushion

of disconnected pleasure still it has worked out something
intimate about your weak dark inside region still as you separate
and click off there is a growing national pride in not being your
actual self but something whole and gigantic and full of salt and
progress and power and clean covered
in oil and travelling ink and passports that go anywhere and
have a long series of numbers printed on them

WITCH WOOD

the witch thinks about what it would be like to
fuck woods and not the government
the stretch of land is green but has redness in the soil
the trees gather around a path from Roman times which
has sunk into the ground an opening flashing and brightening
fucking the trees is giving back the means of production to the trees
xylem and blood vessel outreach tell me how it is when there's a storm
not that different because we all shake but some don't
have a shelter it can't be made romantic branches are entering
different parts of your body
is that right different parts of your body are entering
branches you are shouting loudly and thistles racketing about in
here inside your radical opening and singular throat sounds
for this to work you can't spend more than four hours on the ground
clearing bracken or cutting
because it ruins so easily when it is not a choice the tree is taking

water from you drenching and it has an archive of season
and this is what it is like to feel snow pushing hard in between your legs

cold and magisterial and probably not in any widely available porno
when the summer gets in there inside the pockets of your arms
open sweaty mouth space is being made
that widens and separates more and more and
you look the same but really green hair
you forget the words for assessment criteria for investigation
for intersection for fence for phallus for trunk for
the thing the thing the thing
one solar panel opening eat it up and eat it up
stacked cream layers of light skin just touching the next fine
        membrane of skin
the page with a hoof mark a peaking stain

WITCH EUROPE

the witch has romantic leanings that are expended on no one
apart from the petrol station boy
he gets given flowers and a few kisses because he is too small
    to hunt the witch
the rest of them however would hunt the witch
the witch would like to get some of them under her and cradle
their heads on her breasts or fuck them against the arm of the sofa
the witch would like to have conversations about her favourite
literary genres
the witch would like to roll a cigarette and put it in their mouths
watch the smoke curl up past grey eyes
but she isn't totally stupid
the petrol station boy looks at her tattoo and says 'cool!'

the witch knows all about Europe
in Europe people are sad a lot
in Europe there are excellent things
like fiestas and shaded cupolas
and places that used to be abbeys

but are now mergings between
stone walls and grass and sky
in Europe there are all these bullet holes
from burning the last lot of witches
and there are military parades
where the hats distract you
to a certain extent from the killing element
but European rivers smell of death anyway
so you can never really forget about it

the witch records her body as local
because she's extremely old underneath
the witch understands that just because you stay very still
it doesn't mean you aren't listening
it doesn't mean that you don't exist
she understands that people like fast
so she impersonates a rock and doesn't want to be liked
she impersonates a tree and fuck
she's thinking like a tree
her mind gets green and grows and grows

when the witch was captured they instigated a strip search
they were looking for the place the devil had marked her

with his teeth
or with his penis
or with his own devil instruments
there wasn't anything very obvious apart from a mole
and a suntan mark
so they also had a look inside her
and they did find a smudge there
which the witch said was a birthmark
but no matter
they asked a witch a lot of questions about what she got up to
all the fun she had with the devil tricking people
stealing people's livestock
encouraging women to leave their husbands
turning into a panther and a brown lizard
and having sex with the devil in those forms
they asked her why she hated goodness and life
at which she couldn't help closing her eyes
and thinking of a blue wide light coming off the sea
so they pulled her eyes open
and asked her whether she knew how to make men's cocks
shrivel up
and fall off

the witch tells the petrol station boy about it
on his break whilst they both eat coconut-pecan muffins
the boy has a somewhat flat and unresponsive face
which makes him easy to talk to
the witch tells him about the trial
how there were always lots of journalists there
trying to take photos of the witch outside
and that inside it was quiet and sombre
with everyone in black apart from the witch
who hadn't been given anything else apart from
her slip which meant her skin prickled
at the trial a lot of people made claims about the witch
such as that she poisoned their dogs
that she brought lightning
that she made all the girls in the town go mad
and start foaming at the mouth and downing vodka
that she stole babies and ate them raw on battlefields
that she said war and it was war

the witch tells the boy
that she used to dream about a hill
covered in lumps of earth
the lumps stuck up and so you couldn't walk

properly over the hill or sit or look at the view
under each of the lumps someone was buried
and the earth wasn't thick at all over the dead people
so the witch got on her knees and pulled some of
the corpses up to the surface which were at different
stages of putrefaction
because she really wanted to see their faces
and to remember as much as she could about their hair colour
their bone structure or clothes
or to fish out personal artefacts from the graves
and work out their names
but the hill didn't end and every time she pulled out a body
more stretched out in front of her
so that even those she had looked at were starting to blur together
in her mind
the witch decided that the only thing to do was to eat
some dirt from every grave so that even if she couldn't remember
who was who then at least some of their bacteria might get
        inside her
and so she went along and stuffed handfuls of soil into her mouth
without stopping on and on even though she felt sick and
        knew that she'd never
get to everyone before night came and made it impossible

the witch is an excellent dancer which is good
because as far as she knows it's hard to pin down dance
as a criminal act depending upon where you do it
as its reason for occurring usually has ambiguous elements
also the witch doesn't trust the words which come out of her
which is why she has stopped writing things down
instead there is the dancing which she is good at without
having had specific training and also people expect women
to dance and they expect witches to dance so it neither confirms
nor denies she could be doing it to get sexual attention
which she isn't but they don't know that do they
she dances keenly and quietly with added humming to keep time
you can't belong in there and you can't dance with her
which is the point
it's like that poem except that she isn't the dancer she really is
in this case the dance

the witch has no party membership
maybe because she travels so much
and finds herself interested in things
like a string of red beads hanging off a fence post
in very hot dusty sunlight
peeling paint on a car that has been left to fall apart

weeds creeping through the windshield
and the engine
rows of skulls in glass cases
two men holding each other or fighting in a lit window
waking up in a boat and throwing up the sweet potato fritters
from the night before all over someone's thick dark hair

the boy at the petrol station didn't have a lot of time left
on his break so the witch told him about the burning
the witch said if you could see inside those flames
then you would know that it wasn't just you burning
with your skin peeling back in red open mouths
or your eyelids crackling away in ashy slick folds
meaning you couldn't not look
you'd also know that everything else was burning too
that the sky was melting its blue fat down to black
cold needling stars
that Christ's lungs were splitting under the pressure of
hot blood his words losing their oxygen
and flattening out
that women's bellies were popping open ripe melons
of meat onto the cobbles and high rise balconies
you'd see the small dark core at the centre of the

planet contracting into blank steel
absorbing all the matter and all the light
that you had thought was spread across the universe

spell for logic

you will sit on your hands
the sea has a fat logic if you look at it right
operating sneakily by the moon

you will menstruate exactly when the packet
tells you to

cut off all the dead parts in your chest
a cheap Andromeda
BE ORGANISED

lie on a ring binder and hold your breath
look at the flood of water running up the sand
the snow that hovers
bitchy and quiet

in this rest you are rested
this whole and perfect sleep

tell me what you wanted
from this

spell for change

CRACK

goes the mountain

BLOOD   BLOOD   BLOOD

are you scared yet?

little fissures are putting their black hands onto

the earth

    an opening

SMASH SMASH SMASH

I hope you like this

hot and wet and tired and pain

a bird grows nasty feathers

    its song is geothermal

a clever shaking wound

spell for friendship

utter night with
bras on the floor
and a container ship full

I CAN'T WAIT FOR THE MEMORIAL
TO DO US JUSTICE

the point is she's talking and you don't get it

when the moment comes
when everything pulls back from its sheath of flesh
and the staggering weirdness flows and pulses like
a lash

send her a text

you thought it'd be your mum
but like Christ you renounce
those false and precious things

for a pasty agony

the end of the world (or something)
with who you've chosen

spell for online porn

ok get the camera out

    the reason I want you in this cavity is
       ugly magic

    all the sperm becomes pearl

these   fat   fingers

    the hole gets tighter and tighter and tighter and tighter

       and it feels like a metaphor

    but that's my actual penis

       that's the actual sun coming up whilst we're in it

spell for reptiles

come into the ice!

behind a black eye
the comfort of venom

you are not seductive

you are inside the lithe pouch of self

tell me

how you do that

spell for women's books

the cat shit vellum

    the bad storm coming in over the flatlands vellum

the old murderer's vellum

the poet moves their hips like someone on a tram about to
    vomit

    Athena still and glacial in her blue ice-bath

fresh as a painted door

spell for sex

one damp steak

   hung outside from the porch

whistling into the streaked and furious
night

spell for exile

Ovid

    sad in Romania

   that black sky

  friendly incomprehensible   language

and his own curdled quiet tongue

    COME   BACK TO ME

    the violent sea   is not lonely

    witness

    a furled wrap of your old hair

    lying in the drain

one   fog   at a window

      everyone saying   go home please!

   and the sea playing porous

no no no

spell for Nietzsche's horse

hold me with tender

soft thing

we are all becoming feminine
who can say what man is
   on this nano level

your ears are terrible furred lips

'successor of the dead god'

safe in my crude opening

     good   girl

spell for mysticism

I cannot say it is good when it is so bad
I cannot say hug this guy over here
or   this recording   this nice bowl of walnuts

where you   are

        it all explodes

however

the light tells me something

    one fat scream

SEE THIS

I don't know what yet
   my eyes are still red and cracked
the bits of dust thickening   but

oh

        look—

it is alive out there

spell for reality

what do you do when the answer to
too much is absolutely nothing?
honey sits on the table
fat and glowing
winter light gives you a pass
nine minutes of feeling nearly
completely alive

sometimes the ashy body in the ground seems
to have all the answers
ultimate realness   nasty truth as the final only truth
why then   this stupid relentless yearning for snow
    why the honey and talking

the burning bush is another form of ultimate realness
but what is it telling us
certainly it's nasty
however also   gold
also the entire pocket cosmos shifting and flapping

gentle limbs   holding each other   in the depth of the fire

then   somehow

as   much snow as you could ask   for

wet-gold honey and locusts

WITCH PAGAN

in the little dark
the witch sits
green men on the walls flailing their tongues
who am I but a collapsing galaxy?

when Iphigenia died all her friends were outside
sniffling and rubbing their faces
the slugs inking a black message in the grass
the impossible religion is always to forgive
it is also sitting up to the chest in mud and learning nothing
mud songs sky mud mud harrier
the complete terror of how it hurts
the owls watching you and meaning nothing
the crows speaking and suffering
curling out of the wind with a spit of blood in their mouths
you must forgive that they are not bad and not good
you must not know them and not try
white hot ember sending out movement

the difference is   a space of sky

rope hanging in the uncaught air

WITCH CITY

the fire the ash
something like Byzantium
all the incredible gardens going away
all the incredible sunsets of history
dancing a polka   a shuffly waltz

in a café you can talk to someone and think
this is the end of fascism   right here
in the way that we are knowing things together
climbing the alpine slope of the mind in little jumps

in the café you are aware of Cleopatra   her good headdresses
her astute understanding of economics her carpet rolls
her sense of humour   she is my best girl
she is full of such excellent knowledge

history is so old and gross
wake me up when
wake me up when it really gets started

the city is a cauldron set it off
everything is very dusty
witch's hands are covered in dirt   something sticky

under the streets the sewers is the oily singing sea
in the plane trees there are watchful bird creatures
        interested parties
imagine being so new   not one whole century
        in your smudgy face

a lot of traffic noise
these hurtful insinuations   that witch is all better

    moon with the footmarks rubbed off

WITCH MARS

witch is on Mars
her own occult space program
runes of hovering peace
red blood folds
alien silver trickling down her legs

mars is just lovely
holograms of your face endlessly repeated
witch says to herself that no one has ever been hurt here
impossible! a planetary surface free of bruise
no one has died with wet then heavy unappealing flesh
no one has corrupted mystics still pure and flashing like neon signs
empty red dust   empress of a flat land   cold boulders
sweet tender   terrain of   never - been - slit

from mars
the earth is a small green eye
well   every woman needs a rest
green pulsing   heart   ugly breaker

my darling

WITCH EARTH

the saddest year of my life is every single year
the kirk with its little whitewashed windows
the small towns and the seedy pyres

three girls play in the silty garden
heads on fire with light
their dresses pink and violet
suntrap angels small beasts
always the same beginning
smoke hovering and smarting in the distance

what the earth deserves
so much
so much more
than dead bodies—bits flailing about

when the evenings go dark and no one is about
how do you bear it
how do you bear the small stench

the black water rising and rising

history is hands cupped for some warm urine
girls or people or things in their torn outfits
history is a joke compared to earth
its huge painful promises

the witch watches the girls and their lit hair
their sharp teeth
the earth likes wolves at least
you can give it wolves
you can give it
that

WITCH TRIALS

what happens at a witches' sabbat is
a bunch of women sit together
lock fingers and say things
sometimes they sing
sometimes they tell each other secrets or
make plans
the wind rubs away their voices
they sneak them back
stars cough
this is what it's like to turn over to the devil
so much smoke
so much strange movement
legs open to the sky

the witch has familiars
she has a wolf a dog a sparrow a grey cat
a horse a delicate toad a shivering goat
why on earth would you not kiss those slim
blue tongues

why would you not slip into the night with them
when the devil came back the witch started asking him
about god again even if it was a somewhat awkward subject
she wanted to know why she occasionally turned up at church
and sat alone on the end stall feeling bored and sick and all the stone
seemed to say you are not alive you are not alive you are not alive
the devil pushed his hair up into a butterfly clip
sighed and said it's buried there's just this space
and the witch said tell me about the space tell me what would happen
if I could touch god and lick his marble face tell me what would
occur if I was let down there to find him it's been so long
and the devil said you don't want it but would be something like
black black black black black black black black black black
black black black black green black black black black black
pink

the witch tries to think about how it started
maybe it was when a girl came home late at
night with half her clothes missing
maybe it was when the witch made beds in the cellar
for everyone coming to abort their unwanted babies
and she burned herbs to get rid of the smell of shit
and blood and women went home dazed and elated

by themselves by their strange lightness
maybe it was when she saw a woman spend every day
walking from her house to the top of the hill and back again
over and over never actually stopping
her face was sooty and her mac had rips in it
she kept walking and walking at top speed
and the witch wanted to say please stop
or where are you going but of course
she knew exactly where she was going

maybe it was when she put on that scratchy halter
maybe it was when someone knocked a fence up
and her and the cow just looked at each other blindly
maybe it was when corpses went into the river
maybe it was when the books peeled off
maybe it was when everyone started to look down at
the floor rather than catching each other's eyes
maybe it was when the town board took a financial
stake in sexual services
maybe it was when they kept saying walk don't run
and her legs ached with green splintered clashing
maybe it was when bats fled the church at weddings
maybe it was when there was this punishment

maybe it was when her friend started to say hit me
please hit me please hit me hit me hit me hit me hit me

the witch wanted to run away
but where is away
they were using her name like a flag
hands were grey with smoke
when they touched you it was a
touch that pulls internal organs
dirty shapes amongst the viscera

night can start at daybreak
that was clear
night when you pray and pray
for morning and listen out for a bird's
shrivelled watery cry
and it doesn't come

the witch could only think of it in squares
one small image at a time a sip of it
men standing
cage
neon

floor
foot twisting like a shot hare
colour leaking from a bit of paper

the witch wanted to organise dances
that would heat the room to such an extent
that all of it would be sweated out
all the humanness would bleed
into furry salt and slick pouring
the witch wanted to cut throats
break and break and break and break
and break and break
see what her hand would look like
ripped from its mooring
hate is this spit
it is pushing open a chapped mouth
and spitting into it

the witch thought
once in this square there were
dinosaurs and before that there were these
fish who began rubbing their fins on the sand
they wanted to come up and breathe

and walk around
there were fish-people come out of the sea
gasping and coughing building small shelters
out of pines
at some point one of them will have put an arm
around another one
at some point one will have started singing
the witch begged to the air when did this
what is this

the ash stuck to everything
it became everything and ran down
the houses down people's faces
down windowpanes and chicken
coops and sheds and workshops and
front steps and bed sheets and cardboard boxes
tight sticky little collar around every cell
the ash got into the atmosphere and changed
the weather systems
rain didn't dig out light but brought a choked distance
dogs were eating their young
and leaving the half-chewed bits on the pavement
they know something

thought the witch
the witch didn't record how many people
were called witches or who died
who condemned them or who reported them
who tried to hide who went quite bravely
to the flames who screamed up to the edge of sound
when they were dying who was quiet or
how many children wandered around the mess
what level of society the average victim came
from or what happened to bone marrow in the heat
which people were sent mad by events and started
to beg for themselves to be killed too
who remained seemingly unaffected
what happened to the excess of blood that someone
had to collect
to the individual teeth the gold jewellery the ornate rings
the balled-up sanitary pads the false eyes rolling fondly
the slick waste from intestinal breakdown
the song that she was singing that then ended up in heads
corpse words 'the road the road was narrow but my lover
he fought on' in live heads worming and writhing
the lack of crying at funerals
the boy dragging his filthy dog into the square because

he knew that it was the devil incarnate that it had killed
his mother his sister that it made him touch his own cock
and moan for something that if he could push it up into
the fire too then probably all of this would end
a woman licking at a dark patch on the ground
like it was the most tender spot of something beloved
instead the witch spent the whole time forcing her eyes to stay open
even when the air was very thick she was going
keep having a look
even if it took every piece of eye meat
she would develop night vision
for this long night

WITCH FIRE

the witch lay in immense thick darkness
around her were the bones of the body
she burned
let be burned and slipped off snakelike
being witch the witch still breathed
under the pile of logs and ash
at the corner of what should be known
adjunct to her bones are the other bones
adjunct to her skin are the other skins
and other hair and other eyes hard globules
what dead thoughts can live down here
someone didn't like her husband
someone loved hers and screamed to be separated
someone kept their own shed of goats which they
tended like children someone read philosophy
someone had a tic where they kept scratching
their face someone had had a recurring dream
that they were a medieval knight with clean
gilt armour and their own horse and castle

who rode out on adventures and would
drive through the thicket branches slapping their
face find a damsel tied up against a tree with
long wavy brown hair and when they got close
would see that they are the damsel they are the horse
they are riding themselves they are saving themselves

the witch is tired and at war
she hates the past and she hates the present
she hates how easy it is how innocuous how boring
hates England and wants to stop at that but finds
herself hating them all she hates the landmasses of
Europe their fat seas their pin-tip hills she hates
their verdant grasses and their polite architecture
their binaries their sinewy rivers their flatlands and mud and
     windmills
and factories and press organisations and colonial bureaucracy
     and prisons
and fellowships and barnyards and pump rooms and lochs and
     silage plants
there is light and she loves it coming in from space
clean and sharp as an equation light slipping under chapped eyelids
sometimes warm sometimes cold hint of blue roughness

of spectral red twist of lilac blue rim spot of green
the witch can love light unexpected the witch can feel it
gathering up in itself the light is not stupid or clever
the light is an option as yet unplanned
unknown

WITCH SPEAKS TO GOD

hello?

hello

is this?

not quite

what does it smell like there?

mainly linen

is it big?

well vaulted but tight

are you?

if I

give me a name?

no

tell it then?

ok beloved

do you get sick of?

never yet

can we please?

you must

if the books are all saying?

a lake standing quietly under fir trees

viscous heart

make it up very cleverly

why do you why do you?

this is a difficult one for a whistling void of passion

but I don't I just wait unfortunately

I curl as close as I possibly can

am very disappointing and obscure

then hope

you understand still why we are all so?

absolutely

I am inside that

the line?

ouch

spell for midsummer's day

burn the fire and jump

dear heart

under all this is a centre of human jam
red and pulsing

what you feel touch your face
    in a wavering immense cut

the sun   is hovering at her absolute mid-point

   do you feel that fucked and desperate gilding stir in you?

   your stinking consecrated jam?

     throw yourself down on the floor like a bad dog

get on your knees   and lick the boards

get up again

the fire is doing things to you

that feel amazing

this earth   is so

remarkable

spell for emotions

make a cake that looks like a picture of your mother making a cake
set up an industrial skyline with more and more tender
phalluses hitting the air

don't   you realise   how little   time there is?

you can't set up a portfolio

or reason about the amount of passengers through the border

   YOU HAVE TO START CRYING OR WHATEVER!

   you have to cup a breast just there in the suggestive lamplight
   or put yr mouth on a fox's mouth though it hurts and hurts
   or carry a person on your back over a revered mountain

you have to

   hurry hurry hurry hurry

spell for January

the two-head calls to you

    he is resting over a door and motioning you in and
             sending you out

who will be on your list of the most ambitious fucks?

who will be on your list of the persons leaning towards disaster?

I won't say DON'T BUY

    just tip your head back like an eel is going in

    the cold has something to say   in its weak syllables:

    we will have achieved something when you get up and
           make coffee naked and you are not naked

we will have achieved something when   everyone leans into
    the ugly gale

    and is properly afraid

spell for UN resolutions

the sun comes

they are lying there on the frayed grass

some warm arms and legs

there is only a particular smell in them

small occult fire

when the libraries were burning down everyone was running back
and forth with armfuls of paper

a   touch
down to the genome

SAVE THE

ah because suddenly you care

language and its vulgar rotations

grass thinks too

is thinking:

    'my only'

spell for joy

THESUN THESUN THESUN

nothing can be trusted!
raise up your rinsed hands!
terrible fury and becoming!
take off your clothes!

one colossal owner of the void
brightness folding into itself
again and again vulval or filo

I see a shaking which is total and absolute fear

one day yr gonna die!

the hot impossible apple of
your perfection

you freckled you covered in something

you utter

just open up your face
light's ice cream cone coming
on the inside of yr eyelids

say yes five thousand times
(o love)

spell for political change

a zeitgeist request here
  BE SO IN ACCORD WITH YOURSELF
        THAT YOU GO AWAY

nothing is like you
that picture online
she has a human body bits of it
her eyes and mouth are clammy that's
    weird
there might sort of be breasts under the sheet

anyway you're crying and crying

spit gummy mouth
trailing

she is nothing like you and yeah
would look at your body and blankness
empty

so

take that dead ugly body into your bed
it hates you

let it crack and swell
when things get really bad
lick it
the shaking of pink awful mulch
the scrabbly leaves in the slowly rotting mouth
the river water

are you covered in dry blood fluids
are you sad

yes
adoring what it is
adoring with everything you have and are
her damp alien mess
then you have reached the first stage of what we decide
to call socialism

spell for agency

there is such a thing as a cold and
terrible night

a lot of murdered sex workers

in a drama-documentary about
murdered sex workers

the cold night gathers around

locusts talking about you

things in the air

that are not of this world

STICK YOUR HAND INTO THE GREEN/BLACK SLIME

she wore tight leggings with the band showing

she didn't mind burying the shit back into the
                friendly earth

    a mourner of patchy neon

  is there magic   here?

what do you think

    lady

spell for maths

this is hard

    can you see that rubbing around   the huge cold wind
    numbers making faces in ash

Hypatia had her skin taken off with tiles

    she made equations zero on her long tongue

Hypatia   saw the stars

    but you never will

she saw   blazing signs   codes   the future

    you'll never see that though
    standing in the mulchy forest
    straining your poor eyes

Hypatia got in on a constellation an adorable moon crater
the messages   the decimals   reaching her skinny desiring   hands

    but you'll never see it
    you'll die and you'll never see
    one single thing that she has seen

spell for Lilith

Lilith you look so nice with that snake

    your hair curled the way a serpent might

    Lilith   you are such a bad girl

       i heard you like reproductive justice
       i heard you like staying up all night with your lips
           pressed against the cracks

Lilith can you make an owl demon?
a huge one?
flapping through the night with copper eyes
shrieking for our salvation
dripping internal blood all over used cars and buildings of
    state

    Lilith
you have a really great body

you are a taunt
an un-fucked thing   in a realm of little bits

  Lilith
please sleep in my bed at night
smelling of lavender and coal
rub my back   and look at me   with an impossible black   gaze

the things you have seen
a whole universe of your own making
entirely pleasure   cos yr made of fire

  Lilith
take us back with you

sliding all over the floor
raving & screaming
and very happy

spell for the witch's hammer

a two-pronged sword
to put them down

out there a lot of things happen

witches
undo   each other   a candle in each opening

    witches wake at night and cry
    beasts with curly horns comfort them
    /suck gently

witches go astray
carnality   swooping and fluttering   like a ragged flag

they   laugh so much
covered in purple bruises
teaching tricks   GPS of the eternal flagellant light
    always going home

the witch's hammer sinks into flesh

then   disappears   and only mercury remains   its little
     peasant trail

     the witches eat your book
     then you
     then everything

WITCH VOLCANO

Witch lies on the volcano
amongst creeping language
red spaces/ash snowflakes
lava says something huge
the way it shudders down the mountain
a song without melody
clouds of dust hold the forest
lava still coming in slow sweet insistence
the sun coming in and out of black
waving and smiling with bright teeth

a retinue of ghosts follow the lava
their singing a slow boom
ghosts are not sad which is why they are here
the volcano could never be a sad object
it could never weep only resist
pink lava making heartfelt in a green forest

ghosts have seen things

ghosts have watched aliens making love in silt from silt
meteor love a moon on moon
terrible cell creation whooping breath long dead
but alive alive and crawling with beetle certainty
through the humming fire

the witch has too many reasons to part from the earth but
     she won't part
inside a crater the skin of the earth bursts
she cannot go home from the world
she sees herself warm covered in soot and definitely not cute
a new set of scary words crawling
a new set of tongues that look unborn and haggard

down below things shudder
the volcano is ready at all times
it happily gorges on being itself
as the ghosts rub their hands in glee
as they procreate violently smoke hissing from
gashes in the rock

ghosts are pink and blue and gold   agile birds
they are safe when they can change

safe when they can mourn and have voice to mourn
safe when they can hurt   safe and entirely shattering
all of them crowding up into each other's skinny arms
transparent clever yearning bodies and eyes
transparent tears and happy gnashing lovely teeth
transparent organs pulsing and held out like gifts

the witch watches the charged belonging air
rubs her foot in the salt lava
intimate and hot as god

WITCH SISTER

a sort of woman's face
all gods in it
dearest sister
dearest beloved
marriage comes as knife between us—
we don't need it

witch sister
passionate head and arms
excellent culottes
on the outside can't tell if you'd see it
the way to breed magic is to put our heads together
for now the new epoch appears
passionate cheek and foot
what of 2,000 years for us?
giant churches and pyramids glittering
in a weird unholy air
rubbing our stomachs and laughing   like dogs
witch has many sisters

callous hot mouths
sneaky breaths

yes explosions are good
mountains coming down like pebbles
but also

you put a hand in her hand
witch's hair turns to snakes
terrible terrible
and it begins

WITCH KNOWING

under the strange light
witch watches something strange
moving about
wet dark shape in the snow
hurrier
sentient or un-sentient?
animal or mineral?

witch is scared of ghosts on their own
what exhausting thing might they want?
what annoying painful demands?
what yellow   milk will   they force   through her
sentimental   and lukewarm   wetness

but wet dark shape is not a ghost
is not a thing
is not   in-fact   dark
just throws shadows   about
vibrates lightlessly

in light

witch shouts out an   O

into the hush

wet shape in the sleet   shivers
the very white   day
the   bright mountains
   the long   tepid grasses

wet shape is not witch's soul
it hovers
is not a soul
is a thing but not

one thing

wet   shape   speaks runes
draws in the sky
an inter-spacial worshipper
of   changed positions

wet shape does not call back
but   it does

its huge   call   shakes the witch's ribcage   wide   open

blue and honey

shimmering index   of inside knowledge

wet shape's voice is not a voice

it is a stranger with no body
somehow making the light sing

'come home'

WITCH AFTER

the witch is under neon glow
the petrol station boy is rubbing her
hand he would wear her makeup
he would wear her perfume
he doesn't have a problem with things like that
the witch is sucking a sparkling lemon drink
out of a long straw her hands are cold
time is incredibly heavy but loose holding itself up
like an albatross
with huge ungainly wings crossing immense
distances not stopping to eat or shit or cry or think
the petrol station boy shares a cigarette with her
under the no smoking sign which is his way of saying
I don't know what to be sorry for but I am sorry
the witch permits a half-smile and explains the system
of land enclosure to him while she takes little menthol puffs
she hasn't looked in the mirror for three days and can feel
her face growing into itself
in the car park the devil is waiting for the witch he has on

a green dress his hair is in a slick ponytail his boots
are shiny and dotted with diamante studs
he is thinking about the flammable nature of everything
and how it could still be burned up at any time
even the concrete the plastic files the nanotechnology
and a little part of him is thinking about god as it always is
thinking about the word liberation and its sound
the witch has loam on her cold hands she has soot
on them and bird's feathers
she tells the petrol station boy about what happens
when you agree to go and live in a foxes' den
how your face gets smaller how you do these shivered
scratchy screams how you bite into raw chicken
how you don't do it what you do you do something else
how crows talk to you and come off kind of bitchy
the petrol station boy laughs he is so young that he looks insane
to have only just turned up to the party and nonchalantly
drink an orange juice in that manner while summer is developing
because anything bad can happen and anything can
teeth snapping and cawing blood making little pathways
the devil is shouting something funny over to the witch
the witch is shouting back and she is just shouting
like she will always be just shouting and shouting and singing loudly
and dancing around the petrol station forecourt strangely

Interrogation (2)

How do you do your magic?

How is so balletic, how is like a dance spectacular, getting up
from your seat at the back of the stage and rushing into the
spotlight, rushing into movement, a body doing not exactly
what is 'natural' to it (is dance natural) but what its potential
is, the shapes that flesh didn't command only opened.

How do you do your magic?

If there is a worst word it is nostalgia, the choirs
twisting a larch into a tea towel, if you make it
warm and curling, and so the twitching knowledge
sinks a little, my instinct to stuff leaves into my mouth
recedes, smaller and smaller the incantations and the
freshness.

Have you written your spells down for others to make use of?

aaaaaaaaaaaaaaaaaaaaaaaaaaaaaaaaaaaaaaaaaaaaaaaaaaaaaaaaaaaaa
aaaaaaaaaaaaaaaaaaaaaaaaaaaaaaaaaaaaaaaaaaaaaaaaaaaaaaaaaaaaa

Where did you learn your knowledge of witchcraft?

I could pick any woman, i.e. Iphigenia, i.e. Jane Grey.
Buy a wife, have a nice and symbolic wedding, take her home,
put your penis in there, make some humans. Sometimes you buy a dress.
Sometimes you are sort of kind and have a blond face, sometimes
you are shit, or drown her with one hand pocketed. Inside that, never.
Inside, a slick web. A field of tubers processed under electric lights.
Please record a million, million, million, million, million ghosts.
Please record a system of language never heard before on the surface
    of the earth.

What are your plans for treasonous action against the King and state?

If I say the witch knows things, you won't enjoy. I could smash every
dousing crystal, apparition, rune, astrological symbol, bassinet, globe
of silver, dagger, pleated skirt and we would still. Dogs come
singing like well-born ladies on a good day.

How many times have you used your craft for material gain?

There was once a person I led to be killed. In the ballad it
was four roses on a pale cheek, it was wet long hair like
trailing oil. I found myself radicalised. I found the state I was
in unbearable. I found that violence looked pure, all the clean
edges. When the call came. He was quite small for what he'd
done. I never felt less bad. I was. It was freezing, totally freezing.
Everything was a new country, the way you notice things when
you first visit a city, the half-open windows, the smell of orange
blossom, the bottle-green trams and full-skirted waitresses.
Something after all this time had occurred or was occurring.
Not good, existent. Afterwards my lover put a small
kiss on my mouth and said, do you really hate us all?
And I said, obviously.

Have you attempted to draw others into your dark arts?

The best time though wasn't then, all that dry, agonised
scratching. The best time was a Tuesday, we didn't go
into college. We cut up magazines into strange artforms
and listened to the radio. The sun had the touching innocence
of the early '90s, hair bleached a pale lilac at the edges.

There was a little world and it didn't say anything, nor did it have to perform. No one self-consciously had a pillow fight in their training bra. Instead, our legs got warm. Instead we made mothers into a word as easy as drinks in a bowl of ice. We found all the thoughts there had not been time for in the previous, saw tremendous fleets of new work flood into the hallway. The Odyssey had a bit about periods. One new love poem for each asteroid in the outer atmosphere. Some thawing. All the time I was thinking, I got it back, I got it all back.

\cunt hex\

all the attention & cold love
waiting at the finland station for the trains to rush in
oh
this cunt is a commie red until the very end
this cunt is a commie with its heat set onto surplus value
be as afraid as you can be afraid
be afraid until you tremble the cunt wavering through concrete
so hardly and so softly

cunt hex is the very end of men
it sees you in the small eye
your badly written messages and stink of nerve gas
what is this portable transmission what are these borders
wet and sticky to the touch
blackened tongue parts hanging off porches

the cunt eats ice cream from the clean bowl of your skull laughing
bands together all of the hamlets w/ needlepoint accuracy
cries in the shower cries onto newspapers cries during sex cries

at passport control
cries in the sky down in the pit covered in swivelling happy tar

the cunt has face turned out has lobes switched onto rental
practices refuge with a huge heart in it
please tell me again to my face that emotion has no place
in the body of language
please tell me again why police try and crawl up in this
mouth how it spits them out crisping nicely

a cunt hex is a terrible thing
you are a wet bone in a pool of other bones
you can feel this in your bowels your sunken boy-womb
where snow breeds
it comes in at the root of your spine it is a temple to your
beautiful self pity
it is a temple where everything burns where the body
burns and all the deserving angels
go into the pyre

hex ends your accretion of capital
hex hears you at night the way you fuck— pathetic and nasty
it's both weak and sort of aiming towards violent

we'll stop all that choke your mouth with dousing rods
you thought there was a conspiracy of women didn't you you
        thought that
yes you're right of course
we are laughing at your dick just like you assumed
but for completely different reasons
hex from a cunt is a blue skill

essential as seabirds
meaningful aspect
good work that must be done at the level of dirt
work that must draw all the people together all the workers
all the cunt workers taut and loosening
all the cunt workers cuntless or heavy
all the cunt workers rising up
they will put their program of songs onto the curriculum
they will be herbivore but really nasty really awful
cunt hex is matter of fact
it is excising the bad matter cutting away at what has gone off
your little standards your medley of avant-garde hits
where the world is your emotionless brunch party where
        the world is what you do to it one great
battlefield heaving with unsuitably attired corpses with all

your small type books so ugly in the way of actual plants

we are all so damaged and imperfect we are all so hurt
                know that as I hex you I hug you know that as
you are hexed and the blood is pouring from your head
                and groin that it is only because I love
everything that is alive it is only because after the source
        of the infection being sliced and opened up to
the parched grass it is only then that our work truly begins
        only then that the dour singers get murdered
and you are allowed to breathe

a kind of tender petalled forgiveness comes in my hate for you
a forgiveness that knows how it is to hurt and hurt on
        when inside you turn off
the cunt has its own pink-brown seashell-salted
        brightening solution for all this

THANKS

Jane Mckie, Roddy Lumsden, Alan Gillis and Tiffany Atkinson, for their wisdom. Tom Chivers, who believed wholeheartedly in this strange book from the start. My Budapest family — Dad, Abel and Hanna.

Friends and guides — Kirsten, Lily, Eliza, Kim, Anna, Sarah S, Amy K, Amy B, Lucy M, Nuar, Sophie C, Rachael, Daisy, Rebecca P, Rebecca MJ, Joey, Sophie R, Wayne, Jen, Livia, Ed, Dorothea, Katherine, Eleanor, Rosie, Sas, Lucy A, Georgia, Tanya, Freya, Emily, Bea, Charlie, Amy A, Jemima, Emma, Liz, Sam, Patrick, Charlotte, James, Kelli, Marianne, Sophia, Amy T, Lydia and Kasia.

My amazing brother, J. My beloved Mum, for her support and kindness.

Denise Riley, without whom this book would not exist.

My partner M H, who changed my life, and who isn't scared of witchcraft.